BOOKS SHOULD BE RETURNED ON OR BEFORE THE LAST DATE SHOWN BELOW. BOOKS NOT ALREADY REQUESTED BY OTHER READERS MAY BE RENEWED BY PERSONAL APPLICATION, BY WRITING, OR BY TELEPHONE. TO RENEW, GIVE THE DATE DUE AND THE NUMBER ON THE BARCODE LABEL.

FINES CHARGED FOR OVERDUE BOOKS WILL INCLUDE POSTAGE INCURRED IN RECOVERY. DAMAGE TO, OR LOSS OF, BOOKS WILL BE CHARGED TO THE BORROWER.

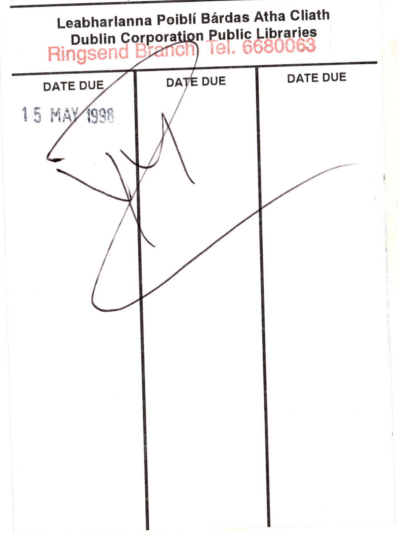

44

MAKING RUGS
FOR PLEASURE & PROFIT

MARION KOENIG
AND
GILL SPEIRS

MAKING RUGS
FOR PLEASURE & PROFIT

ARCO PUBLISHING, INC.

NEW YORK

Published 1980 by Arco Publishing Inc.
219 Park Avenue South, New York, N.Y. 10003

Library of Congress Cataloging in Publication Data
Koenig, Marion.
  Making rugs for pleasure & profit.
  1. Rugs.   I. Speirs, Gill, joint author.
  II. Title.
  TT850.K63   746.7   80–17110
  ISBN 0–668–05079–9

Acknowledgments
Our thanks to Mrs R. Wolf and Women's Home Industries
Ltd for permitting us to photograph the rugs on pages 27, 32
and 42; to Antoinette Jacobson for the punch-hooked rag rug
on page 45; to Lilian Delevoryas of Wetherall Decorative
Design Workshops for the rugs on page 28; and to Noah
Jacobson for photographing the Maud DeLan rugs on pages
46 and 63.

Printed in Great Britain

CONTENTS

INTRODUCTION

Here is a book full of rugs: hooked rugs, woven rugs, braided rugs, poked rugs, rugs of every colour and description. All have one thing in common—you can make them yourself.

The craft of rugmaking is a very old one. It was part of the country housewife's work—and her pride—in those parts of the world where bare floors (or walls) would have meant a draughty existence. The nomadic peoples of the Steppes made rugs for their tents which now fetch high prices as antiques. The pioneering families of Africa, America and, Australia built their cabins and huts and then turned to and made rugs for them. They and their rugs are part of the history which is proudly displayed in the museums of the world.

The men and women who made these rugs would not have classed themselves as artists. Yet they invented designs and colour effects of which many a professional artist could well be proud, creating them from whatever ideas and materials were to hand. Whole family histories in cloth and wool were pieced into those rugs on long family evenings spent rugmaking around the fire.

In our civilised and over-mechanised world there is room and to spare for a craft that will provide not only a useful end product, but the pleasure of creating something of your very own.

In this book we have shown you many different ways in which rugs can be made. Perhaps you will want to try out one of them and, having learnt the technique, move on to another. This can be just a beginning. The possibilities are literally limitless.

1. HOOKED RUGS

General Introduction

There are two basic kinds of hooked rugs: those which are worked with a latch hook and cut yarn to form a knot, and those which are 'hand hooked' with continuous yarn to form loops. The first technique produces a rug with a strong, even pile, suitable for use where it will get a lot of wear—by the hearth, for instance, or on the stairs—and is very easy to do indeed. The second uses a variety of hooks to make the loops which can then be cut to form a pile or left as they are.

In this chapter we shall begin by describing the materials and the tools—latch hook, hand hook and punch hook—that you will need to make rugs using each technique.

Backing

The backing is a most important part as it is the foundation of the rug. You should use the best material available to you as you will want your rug to last as long as possible. Different techniques require different backings.

Latch hook

Latch hook rugs require a stiff mesh made up of doubled vertical and horizontal threads. It is usually available $3\frac{1}{2}$ holes per 2.5cm [1in] and in various widths.

Rya

Rya rugs require the special Rya canvas. This also comes in various widths.

Hand hook

There are a variety of fabrics suitable for use with a hand hook. Basically, you need a heavy, firmly-woven cloth that allows the tool to pass through without breaking the threads. Jute canvas, jute-and-flax canvas and heavier-weight hessian can all be used.

Although some needlecraft shops stock certain backings, we have listed on p. 80 suppliers who hold stocks of all the backings we have suggested and who are well worth contacting for further information.

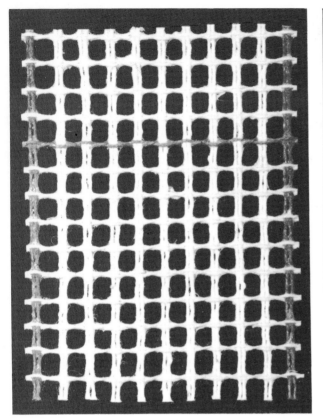

Fig. 1 *latch canvas.*

Fig. 2 *rya canvas.*

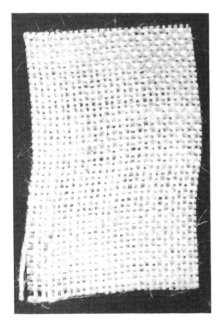

Fig. 3 *lightweight hessian.*

Fig. 4 *10oz. hessian.*

Fig. 5 *jute canvas.*

8

Tools

The latch hook

There are two kinds of latch hook. Both are used in exactly the same way—the choice is yours! The bend in (a) may make it more comfortable to use, but many people prefer the straight shank of (b). The latch holds the yarn in the hook until it has been pulled through the backing. The hook helps you to make the knot as the yarn is pulled through.

Hand hooks

The punch hook

There are several makes of punch hook, each being supplied with its own directions for use. Generally speaking, they can be adjusted to give you varying depths of pile or heights of loop. The depth you require will depend on the kind of yarn you are planning to use. Experiment to see which you find suits you best. Widely used in America, this tool may be difficult to obtain in Great Britain other than from the suppliers listed on p. 80.

The hand hook

The hand hook is a crochet-type hook set in a rounded wooden handle. This may also be difficult to find in the UK [again, check our list of suppliers, p. 80], but a conventional crochet hook will work just as well. The hook size depends on the weight of the yarn, the important point being that the hook should hold the yarn sufficiently well to pull it through the backing. As a guide, a size-8 hook will take 6-ply rug wool.

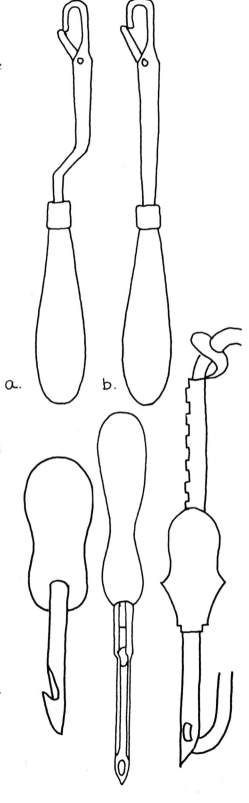

a.   b.

Page 9 rya rug designed and worked by the author. Page 10 top: latch hooked rug. Left: Hand hooked rug. Right: Punch hooked rug, all designed and worked by the author.

Top: a, angled latch hook, b, straight latch hook. Bottom left to right: hand hook, punch hook, adjustable punch hook.

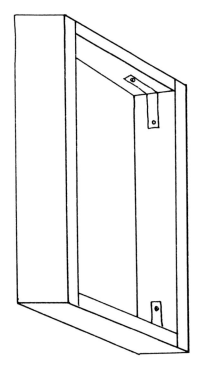

Simple frame construction.

Yarn

In needlework shops two basic kinds of yarn are usually available for hooking rugs: the 6-ply wool frequently called Turkey wool and the special Rya wool which is finer. Both kinds can be bought pre-cut or in the hank. Pre-cut wool can save time for latch hooking and you can more easily gauge how much you need [320 strands will cover three 7.5 cm [3 in] squares on the canvas]. However, it is sometimes more economical to buy it in hanks and cut it into lengths yourself. For hand and punch hooking a continuous yarn is necessary.

It is wise to explore further sources of yarns. The specialist rugcraft suppliers can help here and often have stocks of many different qualities of yarn. Carpet manufacturers are worth contacting as many sell off-cuts or thrums of yarn at very competitive prices.

Knitting wools can also be used but only in small amounts and mixed in with rug wools. Alone, they are much too soft and don't have the same hard-wearing qualities.

You can also re-use small amounts of old wool, washed and dried and loosely skeined. You can even use odds and ends of fabric, torn or cut into even strips (woven materials on the bias, knitted ones on the straight to prevent fraying). For rag rugs, see chapter 3.

Rya rugs are worked with a special, fine, twisted yarn. Always work with three strands at a time.

Other Tools

Frame

For hand hooking and punch hooking it is essential to use a frame. You can buy a cheap canvas stretcher from your local art suppliers or you can make one out of four strips of wood [we would suggest 4 cm [1½ in] wide by 5 cm [2 in] thick]. Either mitre the strips at each end or square the corners. Nail the corners and secure with metal braces.

Gauge

You can buy a small wooden gauge for cutting yarn into even lengths at shops which sell rug wool. Alternatively, a gauge can very easily be made by doubling a piece of strong card.

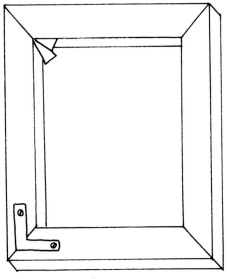

Artist's stretcher.

6 ply Turkey wool.

Sudan wool.

Rya wool.

2 ply thrums wool.

4 ply tapestry wool.

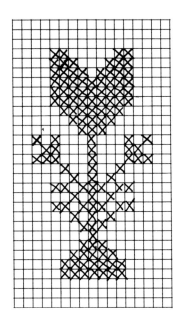

Design

Design is really only a question of translating your ideas into a tidy and coherent whole so don't be put off if you feel you cannot draw. By filling in squares of graph paper with colours you will soon build up a design without any graphic ability at all. Or you can cut shapes out of coloured papers, shuffling them round until you feel pleased with the result.

Here are a few tips to help you to achieve a design which will be suitable for the technique you choose to use:

Latch hook

Avoid thin lines and overly-intricate patterns, as these will be lost in the thick pile. Solid areas of colour in geometric shapes—circles, squares, zig-zags and stripes—can produce exciting patterns. Floral and other representational designs can be used, but for the best effect keep the shapes of colour bold and simple.

Punch hook and hand hook

This technique can be worked with much finer yarn which means that thin lines are not lost and the design possibilities are therefore much wider. As there is no grid to be followed on the backing you can take your colour and loops where you will, provided that you do not try to cross lines of hooking.

Ideas for rug designs can be gleaned from many sources. Here are a few suggestions: folk motifs, old patchwork patterns, patterns from fairisle or jacquard knits, oriental carpets, lengths of patterned cloth, the enormous range of ideas and patterns for other needlework projects . . . starting on p. 61 we have worked out some rug patterns to start you off. You can also find ready-made patterns where you buy your rug wool.

Designs can be prepared for work in various ways:

1 By working from a graph [latch hook]. Each square on the graph can represent a knot. Carefully redraw your design on to the graph paper, using appropriate colours. Keep this beside you as you work.

14

2 By tracing it on to the backing [punch hook, hand hook].
   Draw your design actual size on a sheet of paper. Cover
   your backing with dressmakers' carbon. Place your design
   on top of this and, using a sharp pencil, trace over the lines
   so that a carbon outline will show on the backing. Having
   removed your design and carbon, redraw the lines on the
   backing with a waterproof marker. Keep your original
   design close to hand for reference as you work.
   Alternatively, you can use the special embroidery transfer
   pencil. Having drawn your design actual size on a sheet of
   paper, go over the whole drawing again with the transfer
   pencil. Lay this drawing face down on your backing and
   press with a hot iron (take care not to burn the paper).
   This will transfer the design, *mirror-image*, to your backing.

3 By painting it on to the backing. This is suitable for punch
   hook and latch hook. Paint directly on to the canvas,
   following a pre-worked-out design. Then fill in the areas
   with the appropriate colour.

Transferring design to backing
using dressmakers carbon.

Close up of latch hooking (page 16)
and rya hooking (page 17) to show
different texture.

15

16

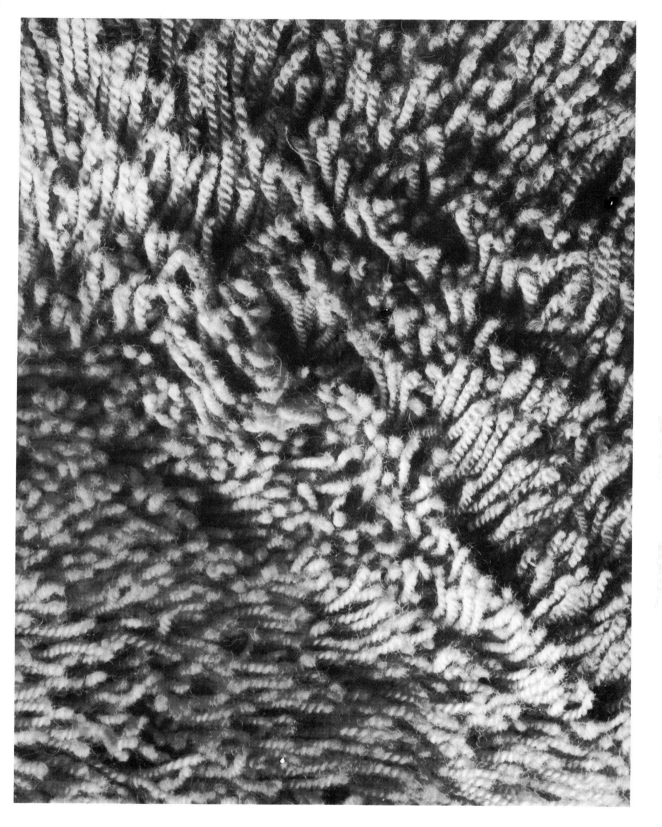

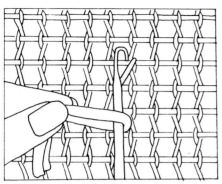

Fig. 6

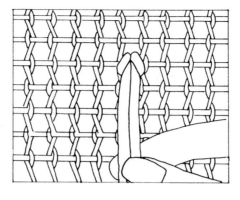

Fig. 10

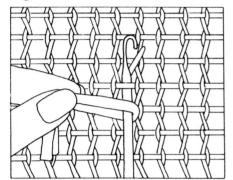

Fig. 7

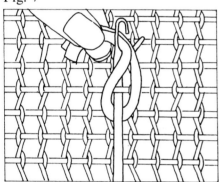

Fig. 8

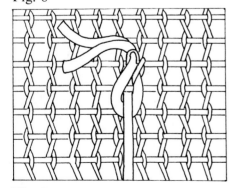

Fig. 9

Making the latch hooked rug

This is a foolproof technique. Anyone can do it; anyone can join in and do a few rows and the pile will look just the same. With your latch hook you will produce a rich, dense pile which is very springy underfoot and will last for years with a minimum amount of care. This technique has become very popular in the British Isles where it has all but supplanted the more traditional hand hooking methods.

Preparing the materials

Backing: Cut canvas to the required size, leaving a good 10 cm [4 in] margin all round for the hem. Overcast the edges to prevent fraying. Alternatively, turn the 10 cms [4 in] under and work through the double canvas.

Yarn: Before you begin cut a supply of lengths in each of the colours you are going to use so that you won't be held up while you are working. Have them lying on your canvas as you work so that they are within easy reach.

Technique: Work from left to right through every hole across your canvas. There are two ways of making the knot: the four-movement [the quicker way] and the five-movement.

The four-movement knot:
1 Fold cut wool exactly in half and loop it round the shank of the hook as shown [see Fig 6]
2 Push the hook under the lower thread of the first square with the latch open.
3 Twist the hook slightly to the right. Place the cut ends of the wool into the open hook and let the latch close.
4 Pull the hook through the loop of wool lying round the shank and push the hook forward to release it. Pull the ends of the wool tightly to make the knot firm.

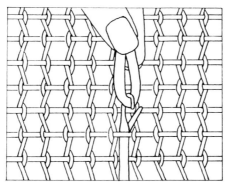

Fig. 11

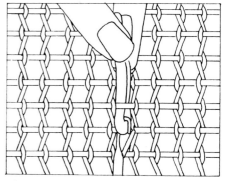

Fig. 12

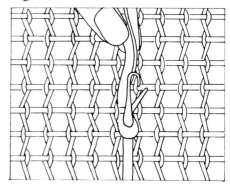

Fig. 13

The five-movement knot:

1 Push the hook under the lower thread of the first square (the hook should lie behind the canvas) with the latch open.
2 Fold cut wool exactly in half and loop it round the open hook.
3 Pull the hook back through the canvas; the latch closes.
4 Push the hook forward through the loop. The latch will open. Place cut ends of wool into the hook, pulling the hook slightly towards you; the latch closes.
5 Continue pulling the hook back through the loop, easing the loop over the cut ends with your free hand. Pull the ends of the wool to make a firm knot.

Use either the four-movement or the five-movement technique, whichever you find suits you best. Do not use both in the one piece of work as each makes the pile lie in a different direction. However, if you have a friend working from the other end of the rug she should use the alternative method to keep the pile falling the same way.

With latch hooking always work complete rows across the canvas, changing the colour of wool as the design dictates. Don't try to work one colour at a time across the whole rug as it becomes very difficult to fill in the small areas as the rug nears completion. Take care to make a knot in *each* hole as you go. You can check your progress by looking at the underneath to see if you have missed any holes.

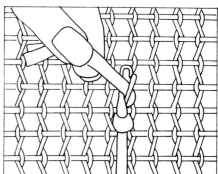

Fig. 14

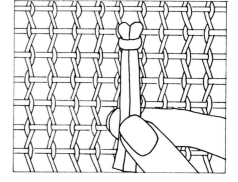

Fig. 15

Finishing

Blocking: As latch hook rugs are not worked on a frame, the work can pull out of shape and so may need to be straightened before hemming. You will need to block the rug to bring it back into the correct shape. To do this, take a piece of board which is 15-20 cm [6-8 in] larger than the rug itself. Cover the board with old towels and lay the rug face down on them. Thoroughly moisten the back of the rug but be sure not to get it soaking wet. Nail or staple the rug to the board, taking care that the warp and weft are at right angles to each other by using the edges of the board as a guide. Make sure that the canvas is stretched taut. Leave the rug on the board until it is thoroughly dry.

Hemming: After blocking, the rug is ready for hemming. To hem a latch hooked rug, use 5 cm [2 in] wide cotton rug tape. For round or oval rugs use bias tape. Trim canvas to within 2.5 cm (1 in) of worked rug. Turn all unwanted canvas to wrong side of rug. Tack it into place. Carefully pin rug tape over the raw edge and to within .5 cm ($\frac{1}{4}$ in) of fold. Using strong thread, hem-stitch outer edge and then inner edge of tape, easing in any fullness which may occur.

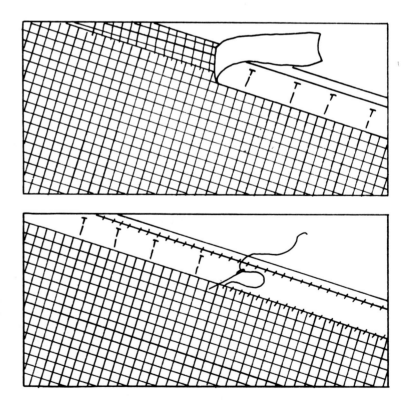

Binding the canvas edge.

20

Making the Rya rug

The Rya knot is derived from the Oriental or Ghiordes Knot.
It produces a rug with a long pile, generally up to 6.5 cm [2½
in] long. Coming from Scandinavia, the Rya rug served
many purposes from a fisherman's raincoat to draught
excluders and pillow covers.

Although the knot can be made exactly as described for the
latch hook technique, a special canvas backing (see p. 8) is
always used. The rows of knots will be wider spaced than in
the conventional latch-hooked rug.

The special, vibrant qualities of Rya are achieved by the
gradual shading of colours across the canvas, and this can be
emphasised by using three shades of one colour within each
knot.

Making the Rya rug.

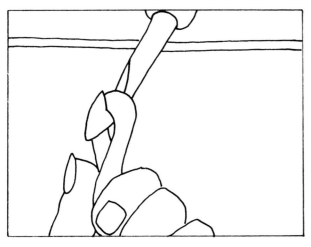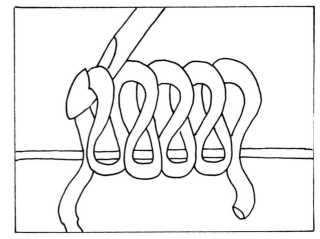

Hooking the wool loops through the backing.

Above: close up of hand hooked rug to show texture.

Making the hand hooked rug

Hand hooking is an ancient method of rug making. It allows for the greatest freedom of expression as you are not dictated to by the holes in your canvas—you make your own. Because you can use both curved and straight lines you are able to create shapes of all kinds. As your technique improves the possibilities are limitless.

This has been the backbone of rugmaking in America for generations and old hooked rugs have moved into the realm of folk art. Britain, too, had a strong tradition of hand-hooking, especially in the north-east, where the materials were easily available from the local mills and cloth factories. A few stalwarts still continue the old tradition, and many examples of old rugs can be seen in museums.

The preparation of the materials is the same for both hand hooking and punch hooking, but since the method of working the hook differs we will describe both.

Preparing the materials
Lace your backing to the frame with strong thread or fasten it firmly with pin tacks. Make sure the backing is taut and that the warp and weft are running at right angles to each other. Allow 10 cm [4 in] around your design for finishing.

Transfer the design directly on to the backing and arrange all your wools to hand.

Hand hooking technique
When you are using a hand hook, you work with the right side of the backing uppermost and hook the yarn through from the underside to form a loop on the top.

With your right hand push the hook down through the backing as far as it will go. Guide the wool on to the hook with your left hand and pull the hook up through the hole, bringing a loop of wool with it. Move two to three threads along the backing and push the hook through to start another loop. The first loop should be pulled right through, so that the end of the yarn lies on top of the work. This is cut down later to lie below the level of the pile.

At first you may find it difficult to keep the loops an even height but by working slowly you will find that you will

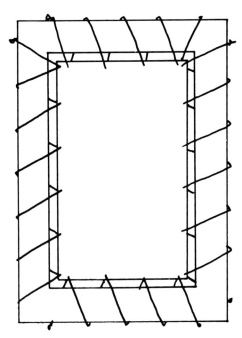

Lacing the backing to the frame.

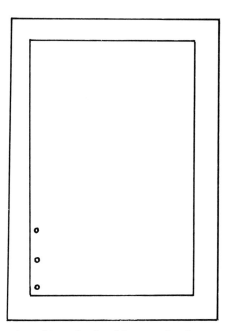

Attaching the backing to the frame with tacks.

regulate the size automatically. A well-stretched backing helps enormously.

If you find you are pulling one loop out as you make the next, this means that you are probably clutching the wool underneath too tightly. Loosen your grip. Start each new row 3 to 4 threads from the last, taking care to stagger the rows.

Do not let your rows or your loops cross over each other. If you are a beginner it is a good idea to start by hooking straight rows, but don't be afraid to try out circles and curves.

Hooking in different directions.

Punch hooking technique

When you are using a punch hook, the side of the backing which is uppermost will be the underside of your rug. The loops form underneath. Thread the hook according to the maker's directions. Unwind a good length of yarn from the ball and let this lie freely on the top of your work. Working from right to left, and with the hook facing the way you are going, punch the hook through the backing as far as it will go, making sure you keep the punch hook vertical. Lift the punch hook up through the backing until the tip just clears it. Move two or three threads along the backing and punch down again. Continue in this way with the loops forming on the underside of the backing. It is essential that the yarn moves freely and unhindered by anything as this is the only way you can achieve an even pile. Do not be tempted to guide the formation of the loops.

Bring both the beginning and tail ends of the wool to the right side and cut them into the pile later.

The spacing between the loops is important as it affects the finished look of the rug. The spacing must be even throughout and your aim should be to prevent the backing from showing through and to produce a thick, dense surface. The spacing will be determined by the thickness of your yarn. A few practice rows will show you which is best.

When you have worked the complete rug you can decide whether or not to cut the loops. Cut loops can enrich the colour but uncut loops do have an interesting and unique texture; so it is simply a matter of choice.

Punch hooking.

Finishing punch hooked and hand hooked rugs

It is important to seal the back of the rug—especially if the pile is cut. This can be done most effectively with liquid latex. The latex binds the rug fibres to the backing and holds them in place. Leave the rug on the frame, making sure again that the warp and weft are at right angles. Apply a thin layer of liquid latex (following the maker's instructions) on the hooked areas only. The latex should not be put on too thickly as this could warp the rug. A too-thick layer will also go through the backing to the surface of the rug. Allow the latex to dry undisturbed for at least 24 hours. The rug can now be taken off the frame.

Trim the unhooked, unworked area of the backing to within 8 cm [3 in] of the edge.

To hem the rug, apply a 5 cm [2 in] wide border of latex to the back of the rug around the unhooked edge. Doublefold the unworked margins and press into place with your fingers. Let the latex dry thoroughly (at least 24 hours).

Cut and uncut pile.

Page 27: Needleworked rug 'Fruits' worked in tent stitch by Mrs. R. Wolf and designed by Womens Home Industries Ltd.

2. NEEDLE-WORKED RUGS

General Introduction
Needleworked rugs fall into two categories: those worked to produce a pile and those which have a flat finish. In this section we will deal only with the flat-finished kind, as pile rugs can be made more effectively using the methods described in chapter 1.

Needleworked rugs are not quite so hardwearing as pile rugs. On the other hand the textures and patterns you can achieve make them interesting and exciting. They can be worked in many different traditional canvaswork stitches. You can use the same stitch throughout one piece of work (see the tent-stitch on p. 27) or you can vary the stitches to achieve an effect of various textures (see p. 38).

Backing
The backing can be any heavyweight, even-weave cloth, but we would recommend that you use a canvas mesh. This is available in various gauges and the number of holes per centimetre will depend on the weight of wool you are using. For example, for 6-ply wool use a canvas with eight threads and seven holes per 2.5 cm [1 in].

Yarn
Here pure wool is preferable, being available in many different weights, qualities and colours, and also having all the hardwearing qualities you require.

Needles
Use large-eyed, blunt tapestry or rug needles. It is important that the eye should be large enough to allow the yarn to pass easily through without fraying. The threaded needle should not be too thick as it must pass between the backing threads without the use of force.

Other Tools
A frame is not essential but it certainly makes working over large areas much easier. To construct a simple frame see p. 12.

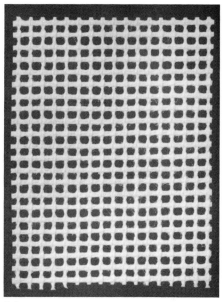

Mono canvas.

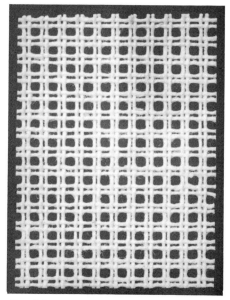

Double canvas.

Page 28: Needleworked rugs top: 'Tulip Carpet' designed and worked in tent stitch by Lillian Delevoryas. Bottom left: 'Islamic Star' designed and worked in tent stitch by Lillian Delevoryas. Bottom right: 'Sampler Rug' designed and worked in twelve stitches by the author.

Preparing the materials
Cut your canvas to the required size, leaving a good 10 cm [4 in] margin all round for the hem.

Design
The variety of design possibilities is enormous. Each stitch produces its own unique textural pattern and these textures alone, used with different colours or even one colour throughout, can produce an exciting rug. Formal designs can also be used and you can draw upon the countless patterns for other needlework projects. Always try to make your choice of stitch work for you by using the texture it produces to the greatest advantage.

The design can be transferred to the canvas using the methods shown on p. 15, but we feel it would be easier to work from a graph.

Technique
Although each stitch has its own working method there are a number of general rules which apply to all stitches.
1 Your yarn should be no longer than 51 cm [20 in]. Longer yarn tends to tangle.
2 Starting and finishing: Tie a knot at one end of the yarn. Take the needle down through the canvas seven or eight threads from where you plan to begin and bring it up at the start of your stitch. The knot stays on top. As you work your first row of stitches this long end of the yarn will be covered. When you reach the knot cut it off. The worked stitches will hold the end securely. Similarly, when you come to the end of your yarn, bring it up to the right side seven to eight stitches away and, as with starting, work over this loose end until it has disappeared. By starting and finishing in this way you will avoid the lumps and bumps caused by knots left underneath and your work will be more sturdy.
3 You should aim to stagger the ends of each length of yarn to avoid ridges forming on the right side.
4 Each stitch should be worked in at least two movements, never one (i.e. down through the canvas—one—and then up—two). When you are working with a frame the two-handed method, in which you push the needle down with one hand and up with the other, can be used. This is a good way of working as it helps to regulate the tension and is fast.
5 If you are working small areas of different colours it sometimes helps to keep a number of needles threaded with the colours so that they are ready to hand.

Stitches

Here is a selection from the many possible stitches you can use. We have divided them into four groups to show their different uses—filling stitches, background stitches and so on. We have tended to suggest diagonal stitches rather than upright ones because these cover the canvas better for rugwork. Study the diagrams carefully as you go and watch to see which stitches share a mesh.

Even stitches

These stitches can be used to block in backgrounds or they can be used to outline different shapes in a detailed pattern. Basically each movement in these stitches is of the same length.

Cross stitch

You can do this stitch in two ways: by completing each cross as you go or by working half the crosses along the row and completing them as you work back along the same row.

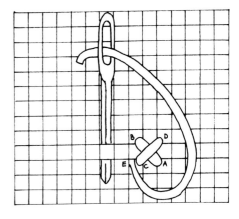

For the first method: working from right to left bring your needle up at A go down at B, come up at C, go down at D. This completes the first cross. Come up at E [which shares the same hole as C] to begin the next stitch.

For the second method: working from right to left bring your needle up at A, go down at B come up at C go down at D. Complete your row in this way. Work back along the same row completing the cross.

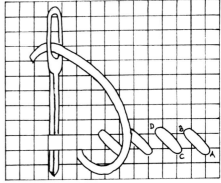

Both methods produce the same stitch and only experience and personal preference will dictate which one you use. The most important thing about the working of cross stitch is that the top stitches should all slant in the same direction to achieve an even texture.

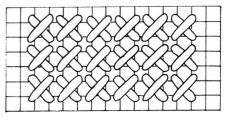

The continental stitch [tent stitch]

Start at the top right-hand corner of the area to be worked.
Bring your needle up at A, down at B, up at C and down at
D. Continue in this way, making a row of diagonal stitches.
When you get to the end of the row, reverse your canvas and
work back in the same way.

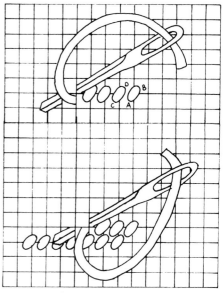

Basket weave stitch

This is especially useful for backgrounds and large areas of
one colour. The stitches are always well defined as the needle
goes *down* into the previous stitches, never up. The stitch can
be worked very quickly since the canvas does not need to be
reversed at the end of each row. Although the method of
working is different, the stitch produced works like the
continental stitch on the right side, the basket weaving being on
the reverse, giving this stitch very hard wearing qualities.

Start at the top right-hand corner and always work the rows
alternately, first from top to bottom and then from bottom to
top.

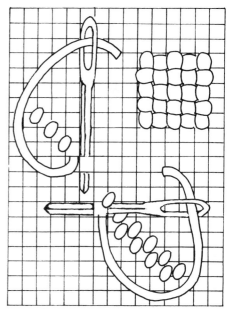

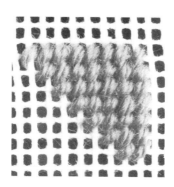

*Page 32: Detail needlemade rug,
worked by Mrs. R. Wolf and
designed by Womens Home
Industries Ltd.*

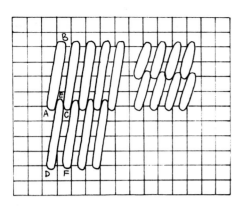

Encroaching Gobelin

This stitch is worked over two or more threads. Start at the top left corner. Come up at A. Go down at B. Come up at C. Work thus along the row.

Second row: come up at D. Go down at E. Come up at F and continue along the row, creating interlinked rows of slanting stitches.

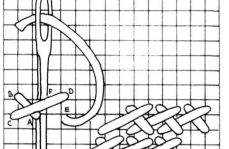

Long and short stitches [1]
These stitches are not generally used for detailed outline, but are interesting filling or background stitches.

Long-armed cross stitch (Twist Stitch)
Working from left to right: come up at A, go down at B; come up at C, go down at D. Come up at E, cross back and go down at F and come up at A again.

Plait stitch

Work horizontal rows from left to right: come up at A. Go down at B. Come up at C. Go down at D. Come up at E and then go down at F, thus starting the next stitch. Continue across the row.

Work the next row starting directly beneath the first row. The lower stitches of the first row share meshes with the tops of the stitches of the second row.

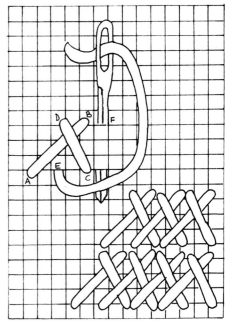

Knotted stitch

This stitch is again a good filling stitch. It is worked in horizontal rows from right to left.

Come up at A. Go down at B. Come up at C. Go down at D. Come up at E. This completes the stitch and puts you into position for the next one. Work across the row in this way.

Work the second row in the same direction, fitting the stitches into the preceding row. Note carefully from the figure which stitches share meshes with the ones in the preceding row.

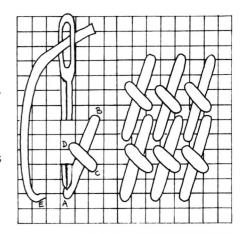

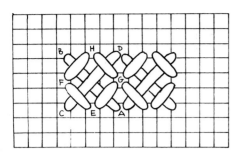

Rice stitch

This stitch produces a rich texture.

Working from left to right: Come up at A, go down at B. Come up at C, go down at D. Come up at E, go down at F. Come up at G, go down again at E. Come up at H, go down again at F. Come up again at G, go down at H. You have now finished your first stitch and can start on the next.

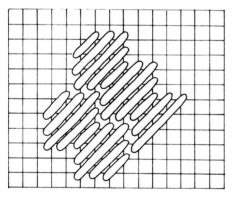

Long and short stitches [2]

In this section long and short stitches are used in groups to create different patterns depending on how the long and short stitches are arranged. The patterns produced are interesting all-over textures. These stitches can be used to great effect in abstract designs where the final effect of the rug relies on texture and colour rather than pattern.

Diagonal stitch

This stitch is worked diagonally over first two, then three, then four intersections of canvas threads as in the diagram. Continue this rhythm to the end of the row.
Position the following rows so that the longest stitch falls diagonally below the shortest stitch in the previous row.

Milanese stitch

This consists of four stitches of graded length. In the first row, work diagonally over one, then two, then three, then four intersections of canvas, and again over one, over two, over three, over four intersections. This rhythm of stitches creates triangular patterns set in diagonal rows. On the second row, the triangles point the other way, thus the longest stitches are set against the shortest.

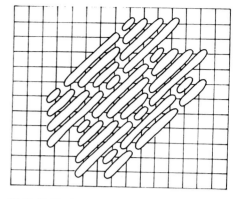

Cashmere stitch

Work three stitches diagonally, one over one intersection and two over two intersections. The left-hand edge of each stitch is directly beneath the previous stitch.

For the next group of three move one thread to the right and work three stitches again. Continue down the row.

The next row is worked in the same way but you start one mesh lower.

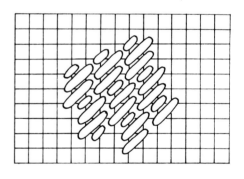

Detail, 'Sampler rug'.

Jacquard stitch

The rows of stitches are arranged to give an even-stepped effect and are worked from upper left to lower right, and vice versa. The lengths of the stitches in alternating rows are worked diagonally over two and four canvas thread intersections.

This can also be worked over one and two, one and three, two and three intersections, and so on, to give different effects.

(Byzantine stitch is worked in a similar way, but each row is worked over an equal number of intersections.)

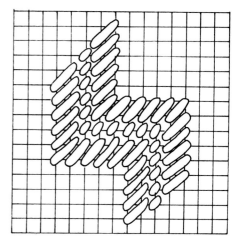

Mosaic stitch

Stitch over one intersection, then two intersections, then one intersection again. This completes each square. Place the squares against each other, so that the short stitches lie diagonally against each other (see diagram).

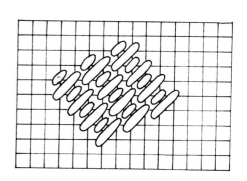

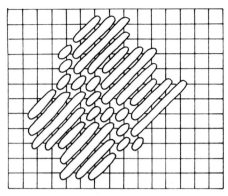

Two-colour stitches

Although we have classed these as two-colour stitches, they can be equally effective in only one colour, see the rug on page 28.

Moorish stitch

The first row of Moorish stitch is worked exactly as Diagonal stitch. The second row is worked over two canvas thread intersections throughout, following the 'steps' of the first row, but using a contrasting colour. The third row is worked like the first row, but staggered, so that the longest stitch is in line diagonally with the shortest stitch of the first row.

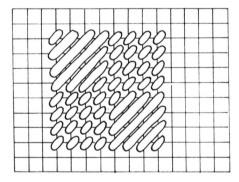

Chequer stitch

This consists of alternate squares of *Satin stitch*—worked diagonally over one, two, three, four, three, two, one intersections to form a square—and *Petit-point stitch*, where you work over each intersection four stitches across and four rows down to form the other square in a contrasting colour.

Finishing off

Blocking

A needleworked rug can easily become distorted during the course of the work and if so, it will need blocking (see p. 20).

Lining

If you feel that a lining would give your rug more body, choose a firmly-woven fabric (such as fine-quality hessian or jute). You will need sufficient material to cover the rug plus 2.5 cm [1 in] all round. After blocking and hemming the rug following the directions on p. 20, turn in a 2.5 cm [1 in] hem on the lining fabric and blindstitch it to the wrong side of the rug. In addition—to make the lining really secure—take a heavy thread that matches the background colour of the rug and, with the right side uppermost, sew tiny stitches through both the rug canvas and the lining about 2.5 cm [1 in] from the edge. A long and short stitch is best for this, that is, a short stitch on the right side and a long stitch on the underside. Finish off neatly.

3. RAG RUGS

General Introduction

One of the most interesting rugs is the rag rug made from every imaginable scrap of fabric. For hundreds of years people have been making these rugs in their homes. Thrifty people, used a variety of techniques to achieve mats and coverings that have all the interest of family history woven or knotted into their surfaces, in much the same way as the patchwork quilt: a piece of Dad's trousers here, a scrap of Great-aunt's petticoat there. You can trace the contributions if you look closely, but worked into the rug they start a new life of their own.

Preparing the materials

If you are a beginner, don't use lots of different kinds of material in the same rug. Choose one kind of material, say wool, cotton or man-made fibre of some kind. Whatever you choose should be of a medium or heavy weight if the rug is to get much wear. Should you prefer to use new material why not write to cloth manufacturers for remnants? This is a much more economical way of tackling the problem than buying straight from a retail store. Or you can have a mixture of old and new. There are all kinds of different ways of getting old cloth—your own old clothes, your friends' old clothes, jumble sales, the colours do not really matter. You will soon sort them all out and plan them into your rug. However, closely-woven fabrics are better—knitted fabrics such as jersey should be avoided as they are too flexible.

The first thing to do is to wash your rags and pieces, remembering to pull down hems, unpick darts and so on. Then sort them into roughly different-coloured piles to give you an idea of what you have. This is particularly helpful for any of the hooking methods, the pen-wiper and the woven rugs, but not so important for the others as these can rely on random effects for their main impact.

Opposite, needleworked rug 'Butterflies' worked by Mrs. R. Wolf and designed by Womens Home Industries Ltd.

Since the different techniques have varying requirements as to length and width we shall discuss cutting in each individual section, but bear in mind that lighter-weight fabrics should be cut wider than the heavier ones if you are mixing weights, to achieve the same bulk. Using our measurements only as a guide, experiment with your cloth until you get the effect you require.

Latch hook rugs

Cut up your rag into bias strips of 11.5 to 12.5 cm [4½–5 in] long and 1.5 cm [½ in] wide. A canvas backing ten holes to 8 cm [3 in] is highly suitable. (See latch canvas p. 8.)

Follow the technique for latch hooking wool, but hook into every other row as the rag may become too tightly packed if you hook into every row.

After ten rows check the effect and, if it looks a bit flimsy, go back and fill in the unhooked rows. Then continue hooking into every row. You want the finished pile to be thick and close. Finish off as you would for wool.

Hand hooked and punch hooked rugs

For a tight, hard-wearing rug, cut bias strips 1.5 cm [½ in] wide from medium-weight material. You may find that the strips need to be cut narrower for the punch hook technique as they must flow smoothly through. Since you require a continuous length cut your strips as long as you can, rolling them into balls.

The technique for working these rugs is, again, like that for wool. We recommend the same kind of backing, too. (p. 8.) Experiment with the height of loop until you find the right height for the kind of fabric you are using. Remember that you will have to work at least two or three rows before you can judge the final effect. The pile can be left looped or cut.

Page 45 top left: punch hook rug, designed and worked by Antoinette Jacobson. Top right: poked rug. Bottom left: latch hook rug. Bottom right: 'Frisant rug' designed and worked by the author.

Page 46: braided rug, designed and worked by Maude DeLan.

Page 47: close up of punch hooked (top), latch hooked (bottom left) and poked (bottom right) rugs, to show textures.

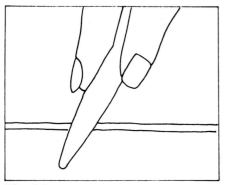
Fig. 16

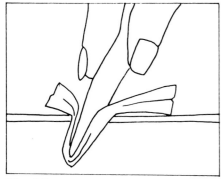
Fig. 17

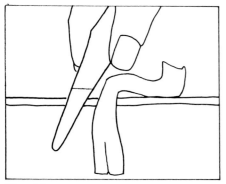
Fig. 18

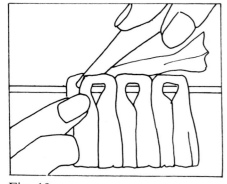
Fig. 19

Poked rugs

This is a very old technique, using the simplest of tools—a round-pointed peg—to make the holes through which to poke the rags. Any tool can be used which will make a hole in the backing without breaking the threads, for example, a carpenter's awl or bodger, a whittled-down clothes peg, a large wooden knitting needle, etc. The backing should again be hessian, and you can use any weight of material to produce a dense pile.

Technique

Cut the hessian to size, allowing 5 cm [2 in] all round for finishing. Stretch the hessian on to a frame as described on p. 23. However, if you are only making a small rug this can quite easily be worked on your knee. As with punch hooking, you work with the wrong side of the rug on top and the pile is produced underneath.

Cut the fabric into bias strips. The strips should be 4 × 10 cm [1½ × 4 in].

Take the peg and poke a hole, working from the top downwards. With your peg push one end of the strip through to the underside. Pull it gently until it is just under halfway through. Poke another hole in the backing about four threads along, and poke in the other end of the strip. Make sure that the ends of the strip are even on the right side. Take the next strip of fabric and poke it into the same hole as the last one. Make another hole four threads along and poke in the other end. Continue double pegging in this way along the row. The next row should be about four threads away from the first row, but check that you are getting the right density after a few rows.

When you have completed your poking, finish off as in punch hooking. (See page 26.)

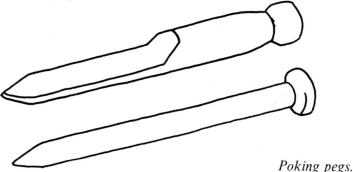
Poking pegs.

Braided rugs

Braided rugs cost virtually nothing. All you need are rags and a needle and thread. The preparation is lengthy, but the effects created are so individual they are well worth the effort. Do read all the instructions for preparation before you start so that you can get a clear picture of what you are doing.

Once again, medium or heavyweight fabrics are best.

Cutting:

Cut the fabric into 5-10 cm [2-4 in] wide strips, depending on the weight (heavy fabrics should be cut narrower than lighter ones).

Joining the strips

The strips should be joined together to form 315-366 cm [10-12 ft] lengths.

Folding the strips

The raw edges must be hidden. Fold the strips so that the raw edges meet in the middle.

Then fold them in half again. Roll the strips into balls.

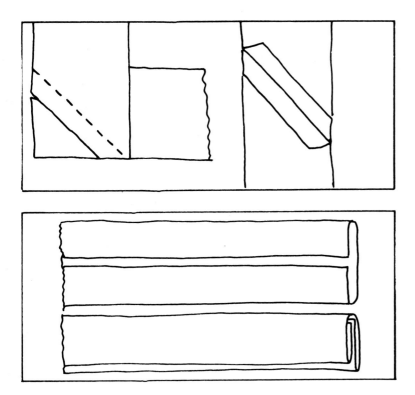

Top: joining the strips. Bottom: folding the strips.

49

Braiding

To begin braiding, unwrap about 122 cm [4 ft] from each of three balls. Join two strips on the bias, then place the third strip across to form a T.

Tack the third strip into place to hold it firmly. Put the joined ends under a weight—a heavy book perhaps—to secure them while you braid.

Many of us will remember braiding our hair as children. The principle is just the same. Bring the left strip over the middle strip, bring the right strip over the new middle strip, and so on. Keep the tension as even as possible. Stitch new strips to the working strips as necessary. Try and stagger the seams to avoid lumps.

Making up the rug

We suggest you start by making a round rug as this is the easiest to do. To avoid getting in a tangle you should work the braids into shape and stitch them as soon as you have sufficient length. Take the joined end of braid and start coiling it into a flat circle. Be sure to keep the shape circular all the time you are working the rug.

Making the 'T' join.

Starting to braid.

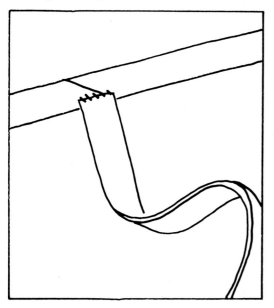
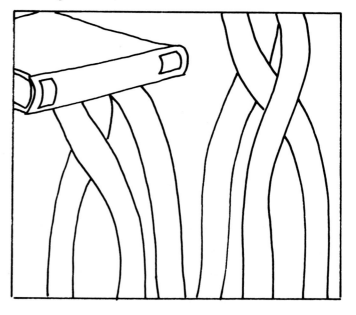

Sewing the braids

Using a carpet needle and a heavy-linen carpet thread, sew first through the loop of one braid and then through the loop lying beside it.

Work back and forth between the braids, taking care that they remain flat and that the stitching is firm but not too tight. Continue until your rug reaches its final size.

Tapering

To achieve a smooth finish on the edge of the rug taper the last 46 cm [18 in] of each strip to about half normal width. Finish the braiding and slip the tapered ends into the loop lying beside them. Secure in place, hiding the raw edges.

Squares, ovals and rectangles

These shapes are easy to make by following the working drawings below.

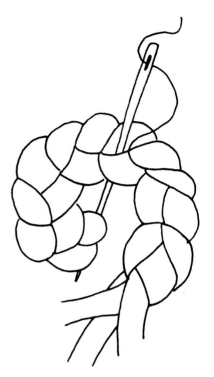

Above: starting the coil.

Below: sewing the braids together.

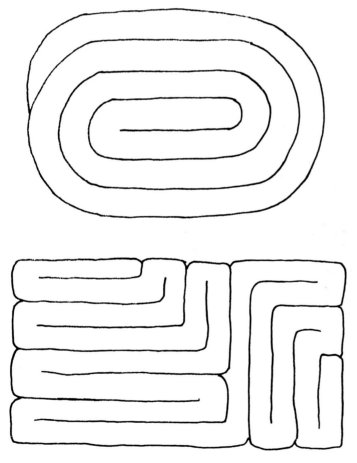

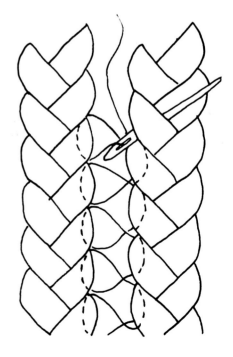

Square and oval coiling.

Pen-wiper rugs

This is a very individual technique which comes from America. The rug consists of layered concentric circles of fabric sewn to a strong backing. Beautiful effects can be achieved by a careful balancing of the colours.

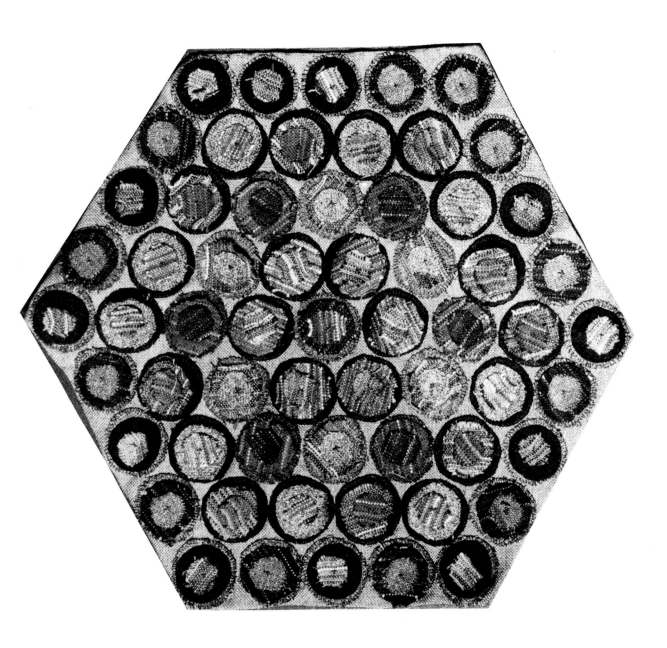

Left: close up of braided rug. Here the braids have been sewn flat against each other producing an interesting and individual effect.

Above: penwiper rug.

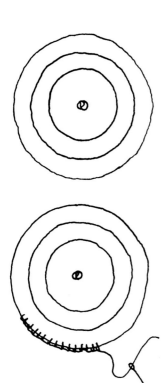

Technique

Cut your backing—which should be a heavy hessian or monk's cloth—to the required size, leaving 10 cm [4 in] round the edge for finishing. Choose a medium, to heavy-weight, material that doesn't easily fray. Cut your fabric into circles of varying size, say 2.5 cm [1 in], 4 cm [1½ in] and 5 cm [2 in] in diameter. Join the three circles together through the centres with a french knot or firm cross-stitch.

Attach each finished group to the backing using blanket or buttonhole stitch. Place the circles so that they just touch each other, allowing the minimum of backing to show through. It is a good idea to prepare all your circles first and lay them out into the pattern. When you have finished sewing the circles to the backing turn under the raw edge of the backing and line your rug with another layer of monk's cloth or hessian. (See p. 41.)

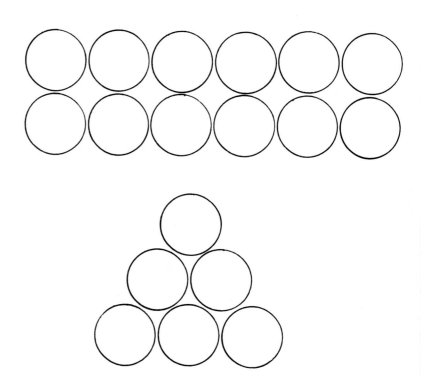

Above: sewing the circles together.
Right: two ways to arrange the finished circles.

54

Woven rugs

Weaving is an ancient craft and can be one of the most complicated techniques, involving expensive equipment and tools. However, very good effects can be obtained from a simple box loom and the collection of scraps in your ragbag.

The box loom

The box loom can be easily made up from two pieces of wood measuring 5 × 10 × 122 cm [2 × 4 × 48 in] and two more 5 × 10 × 152.5 cm [2 × 4 × 60 in]. Lay these out in a rectangle, butting the corners. Secure the corners with metal braces, making sure that the rectangle is true.

This size is suitable for making a rug up to 91.5 × 152.5 cm [3 × 5 ft]. If you want to make a smaller rug, reduce the size of the frame.

Shuttle

A large-eyed tapestry needle can be used, but you will find the work much easier if the fabric is first wound on to a shuttle. You can easily make one out of a flat piece of wood with a knotch cut out of each end. Alternatively, wind the strips into a ball.

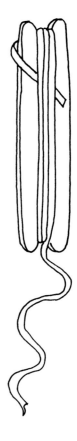

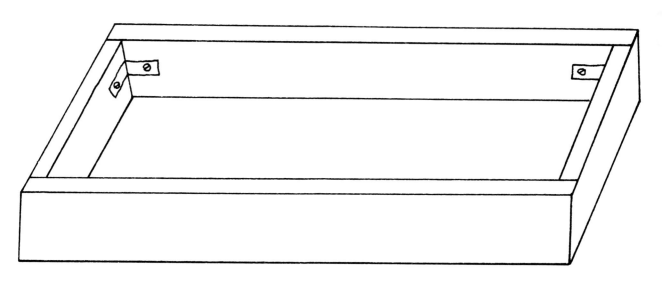

The box loom.

Preparing the loom

To prepare the loom for working, mark the centre point of each short side. Measure and mark 15 cm [6 in] from each end of the short sides.

For the warp [the long threads running from top to bottom] you should use a good strong carpet thread but any very strong heavy-duty thread [strong string for example] will do. Tie one end of the thread at the point of one of the 15 cm [6 in] marks. Take the thread up to the 15 cm mark on the opposite end. Take it round the wood and bring it back to the the starting point in figure-of-eight fashion.

Continue working figures-of-eight in this way, making sure as you go that the warp thread is tight, until you have worked 200 turns. You will have made 400 warp threads across 92 cm [36 in]. If you are using a smaller loom, reduce the number of warp threads, keeping the total number divisible by four.

Knot the ends of the warp threads together when necessary. The knots will be covered by the fabric as you weave. Secure the end of the last warp to the frame with a knot. The loom is now ready for working.

Next prepare the fabric for the weft as for braiding, rolling the strips into balls ready for use. (See p. 49.)

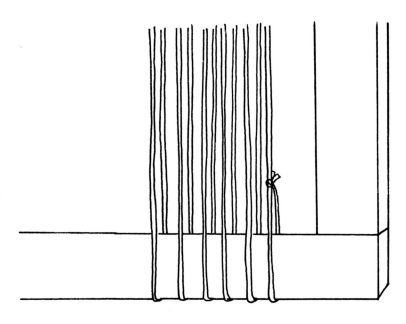

Winding the warp.

56

Start weaving

To start weaving with the strips, thread one end of the strip into your large-eyed tapestry needle (or wind it on to your shuttle). Beginning at the lower right-hand side, weave under four threads and over four threads and so forth along the row, leaving about 15 cm [6 in] of the strip dangling. This will be worked in later. Make this first row as straight as possible because it will affect the rest of the rug. The second row is worked from left to right, going over the threads you went under in the first row and under those you went over. These two rows are repeated throughout the whole rug. You should keep the warps evenly spaced as you work. Beat each row down firmly with your fingers as you work to prevent gaps between the rows. The tension of the rows must be even to prevent a waist from forming at the centre. Any joins in the fabric strips must be made away from the edges so that the rug is kept stable. Finish the last row about 15 cm [6 in] from the edge. Work the 15 cm end left dangling at the beginning into the rug.

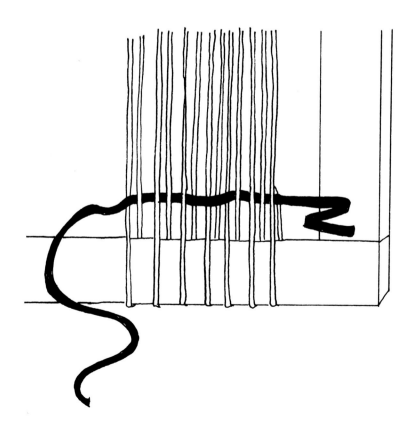

Starting to weave the rags.

Remove the rug from the loom by carefully cutting the warp threads in the following way: cut the first two groups of four and join the first four to two of the second four; then the other two of the second four will be joined to the following two [see diagram]. Cut and tie as you go. Do not cut all the warps together. Trim the ends to neaten.

Woven rugs may be worked in one colour but weaving in bands of different colours is much more interesting and the resulting rug far more exciting.

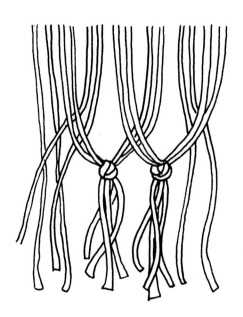

Tying the cut warp to finish.

Opposite: close up of frisant, braided and woven rugs to show different textures.

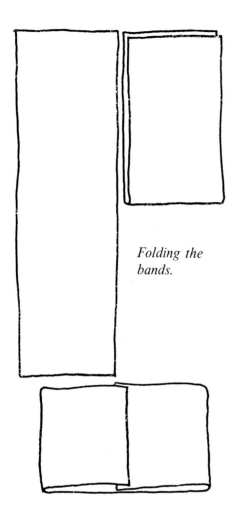

Folding the bands.

The 'Frisant' Rug from France

This rug is made up of a multitude of little bands of fabric, folded in half and sewn row after row on to a hessian or jute backing. This is an excellent way to use up all those odd scraps of lighter weight fabric—printed cottons, ginghams and solids —that might not be suitable for other methods of rugmaking.

Technique
Cut the backing to size, allowing 8 cm [3 in] all round for the hem. Turn the hem in and finish with rug tape as described on page 20. Cut the fabrics along the grain with pinking shears (to reduce fraying) into bands 10 × 4 cm [3¾ × 1½ in]. Pin or tack the first row of bands into place along the edge of the finished backing. Each should overlap the edge by about 2 cm [½ in] and they should just overlap each other along the row as in the diagram. Machine or hand stitch along the row about halfway down the bands. Pin and tack the second row into place so that the bands just overlap the first row of stitches. The second row of bands should overlap the first row brick fashion. Continue to lay and stitch further bands in this way along the length of the rug. To give a neater edge to the last row of bands fold them slightly differently. Fold each short end to the middle of the band and then lay the bands along the edge of the rug as before and sew them into place. The raw edges on the short ends will now be tucked away out of sight. Line the rug with hessian as described on page 41.

Laying out the bands.

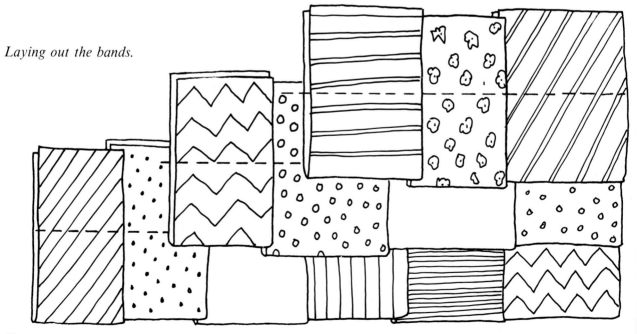

SOME RUG
DESIGNS

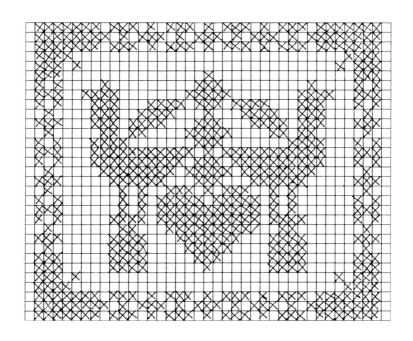

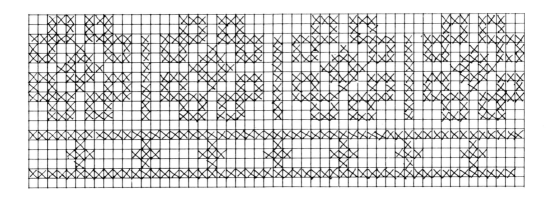

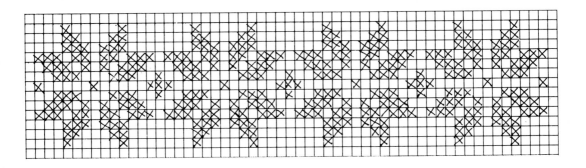

Cross·stitch motifs from old samplers

Opposite: hand hooked rag rug designed and worked by Maude DeLan.
Overleaf-top: penwiper rug designed and worked by the author.
Bottom: woven rug from the Allgau region of Germany.

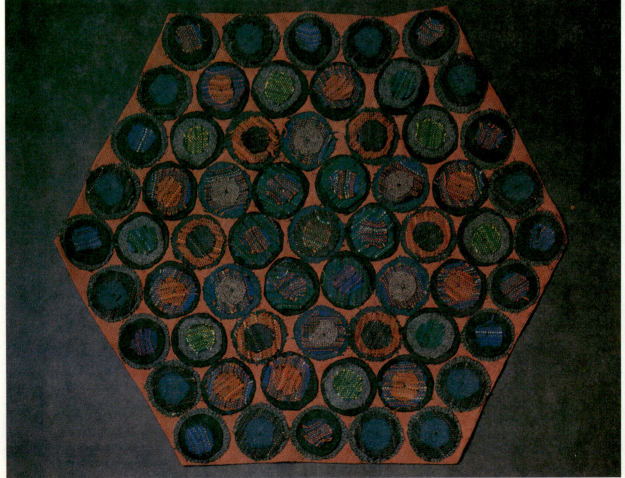

2 motifs for punch/hand hook

punch hook

66

hand hook

punch/hand, poke

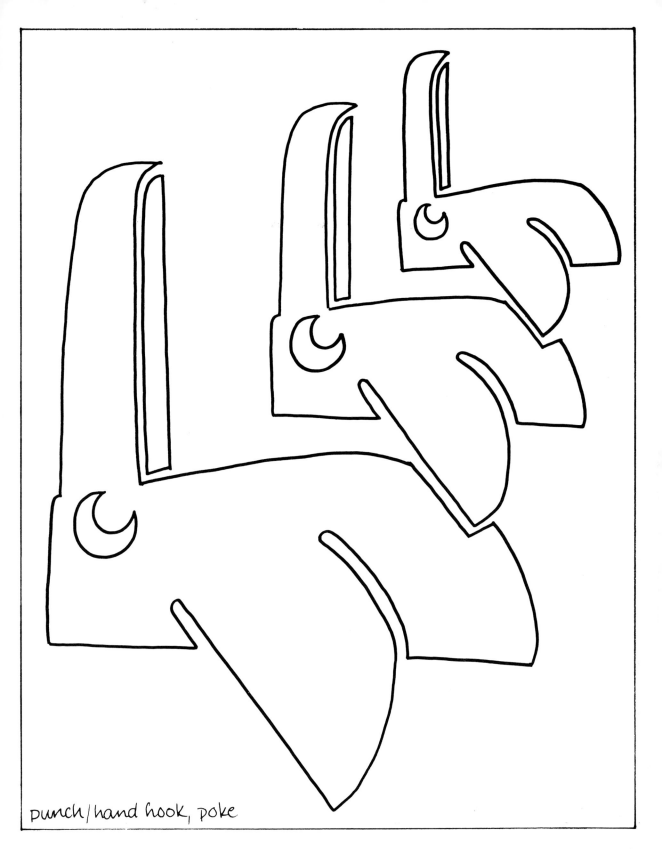

punch/hand hook, poke

69

punch|hand hook poke

punch/hand hook, poke

71

punch/hand hook, poke

punch/hand hook, poke

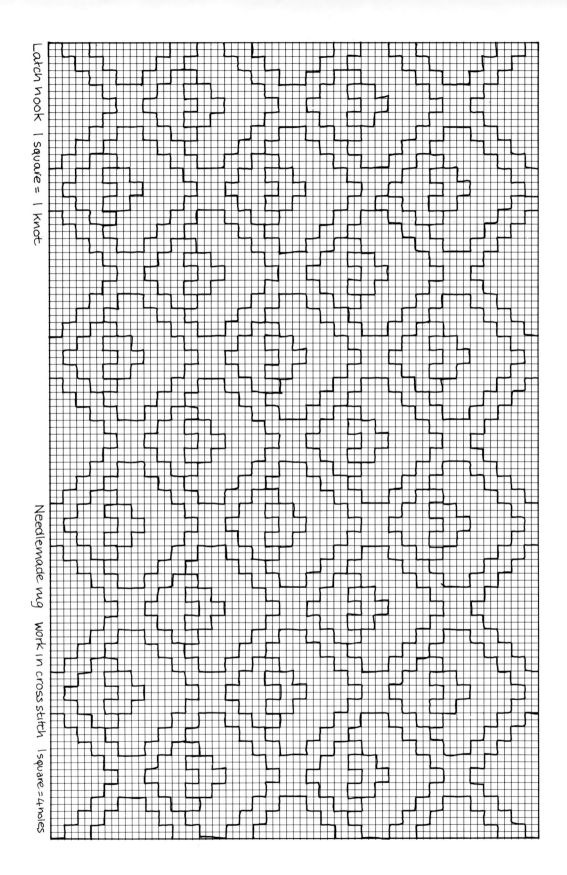

Latch hook   1 square = 1 knot

Needlemade rug   work in cross stitch   1 square = 4 holes

74

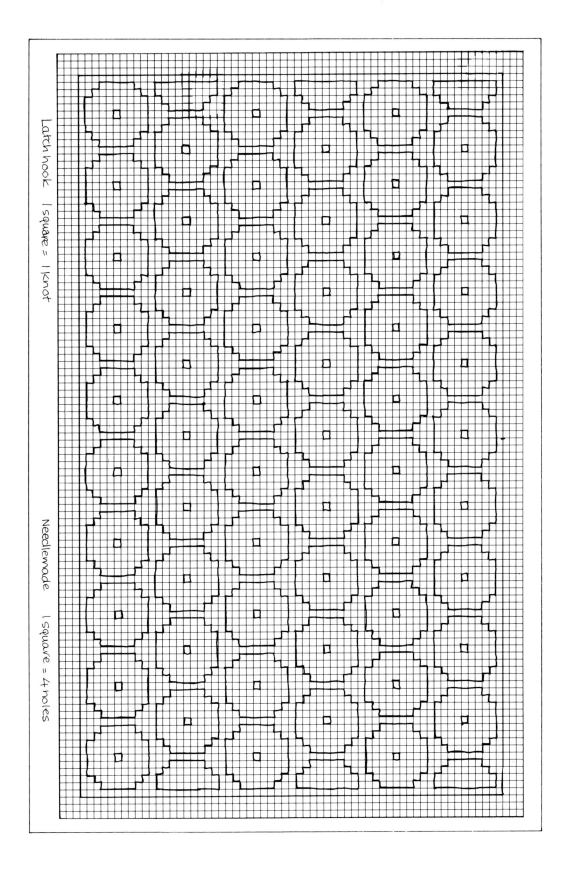

Latch hook   1 square = 1 knot

Needlemade   1 square = 4 holes

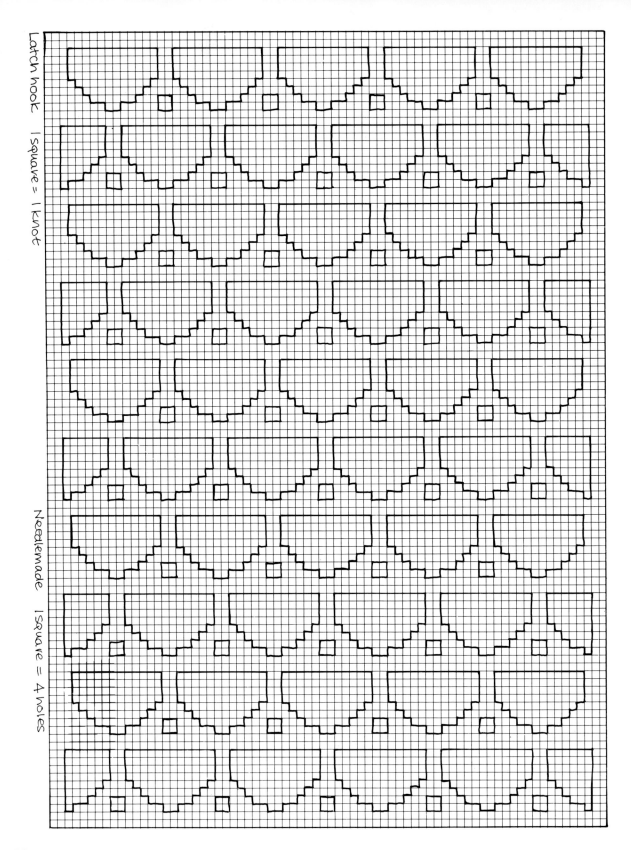

Latch hook   1 square = 1 knot

Needlemade   1 square = 4 holes

76

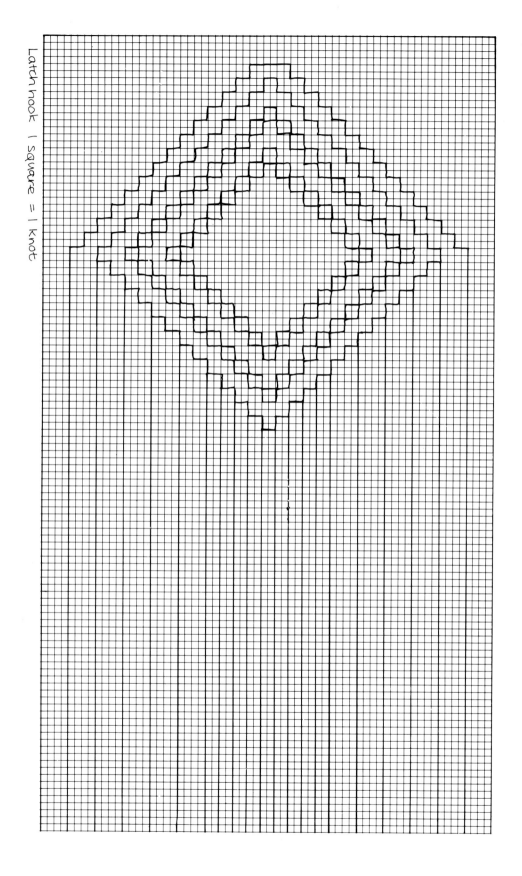

Latch hook 1 square = 1 knot

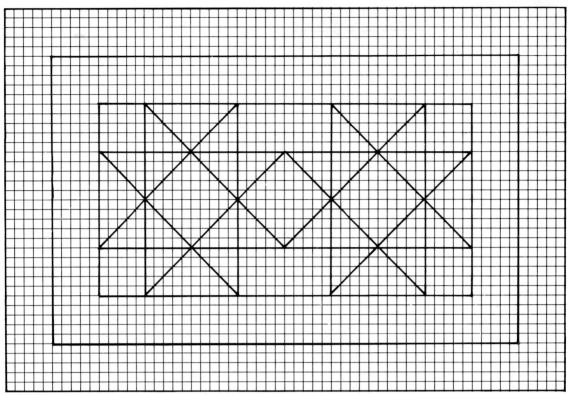

Latch hook   1 square = 2 knots

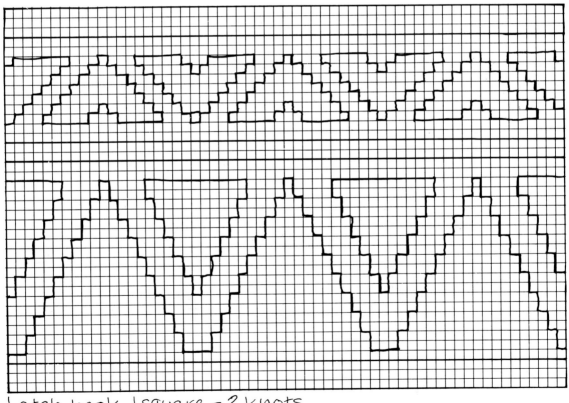

Latch hook 1 square = 2 knots

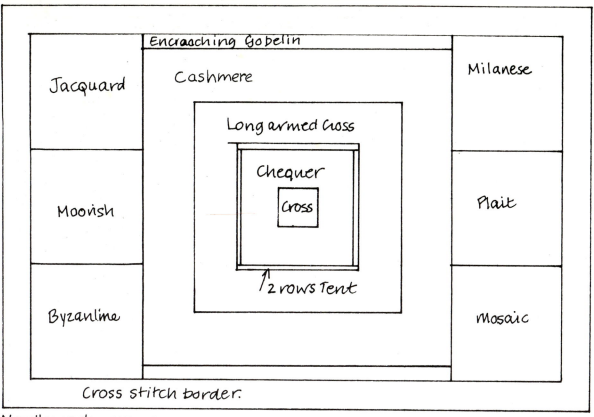

Encroaching Gobelin

Jacquard

Cashmere

Milanese

Long armed Cross

Chequer

Cross

Moorish

Plait

↑ 2 rows Tent

Byzantine

Mosaic

Cross stitch border.

Needlemade rug page

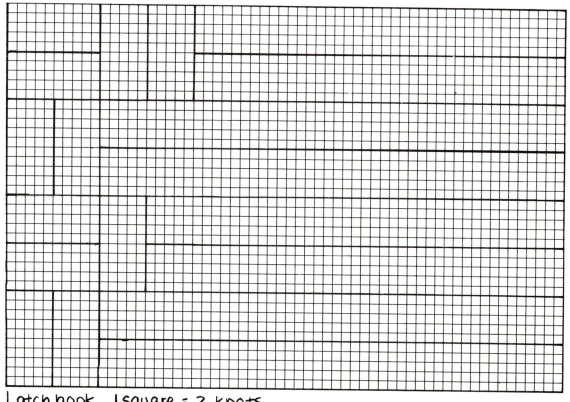

Latch hook   1 square = 2 knots

SUPPLIERS

RUG YARNS

SPINNERIN YARN CO. INC
230 Fifth Avenue, New York NY10001
Write for local stockists

WOOL DESIGN INC
8916 York Road, Charlotte, NC28210
Write for local stockists

PATERNAYAN BROS. INC
312 East 95th Street, New York NY10028
Write for local stockists

YARNS AND CANVASSES

ART NEEDLEWORK TREASURE TROVE
Box 2440 Grand Central Station, New York NY10017
Write for local stockists

ALL MATERIALS FOR RAG RUGS

BRAID AIDS
466 Washington Street, Pembroke MA02359
Write for catalog of all rug making supplies including
punch needles, hand hooks, latch hooks and backings